D1607259

EXPLORING DINOSAURS & PREHISTORIC CREATURES

TROODON

By Susan H. Gray

THE CHILD'S WORLD®
CHANHASSEN, MINNESOTA

Published in the United States of America by The Child's World®
PO Box 326, Chanhassen, MN 55317-0326
800-599-READ
www.childsworld.com

Content Adviser: Peter Makovicky, PhD, Curator, Field Museum, Chicago, Illinois

Photo Credits: The Academy of Natural Sciences of Philadelphia, Ewell Sale Stewart Library: 16, 17; American Museum of Natural History Library: 6 (# 21714-02, Rick Edwards), 11 (# 296563), 13 (#2A1653), 14 (neg 28973); Scott T. Smith/Corbis: 15; Layne Kennedy/Corbis: 19; Jonathan Blair/Corbis: 24; Denis Scott/Corbis: 27; Rich Frishman/Time Life Pictures/Getty Images: 8; Laski Diffusion/EastNews/Liaison/Getty Images: 23; Disney Enterprises/Getty Images: 26; The Natural History Museum, London: 5, 7, 9, 22, 25; Christian Darkin/Science Photo Library/Photo Researchers, Inc.: 20; Courtesy of the Peabody Museum of Natural History, Yale University, New Haven, CT: 21.

The Child's World®: Mary Berendes, Publishing Director

Editorial Directions, Inc.: E. Russell Primm, Editorial Director; Katie Marsico, Associate Editor; Ruth Martin, Line Editor; Judith Shiffer, Assistant Editor; Matt Messbarger, Editorial Assistant; Susan Hindman, Copy Editor; Melissa McDaniel, Proofreader; Olivia Nellums, Fact Checkers; Tim Griffin/IndexServ, Indexer; Dawn Friedman, Photo Researcher; Linda S. Koutris, Photo Selector

Original cover art by Todd Marshall

The Design Lab: Kathleen Petelinsek, Design and Page Production

Library of Congress Cataloging-in-Publication Data
Gray, Susan Heinrichs.
Troodon / by Susan H. Gray.
v. cm. — (Exploring dinosaurs)
Includes bibliographical references and index.
Contents: Dad brings home a meal—What is a Troodon?—Who found the first Troodon?—What did Troodon do all the time?—Eggs by the dozens—What became of Troodon?
ISBN 1-59296-238-6 (lib. bdg. : alk. paper) 1. Troodon—Juvenile literature. [1. Troodon. 2. Dinosaurs.] I. Title.
QE862.S3G69567 2005
567.912—dc22 2003026988

TABLE OF CONTENTS

CHAPTER ONE

Dad Brings Home a Meal

The sun disappeared behind the hills. Purple streaks reached across the evening sky, and a few stars twinkled overhead. On the ground, the shadows lengthened and crept over the awakening *Troodon* (TROH-uh-don). *Troodon* slowly stood up and stretched his neck. He wiped a rough hand across his face and shook his head.

Just then he heard a soft rustling sound. He turned his head, and in the dim light he spotted a big, ratlike animal nosing around the ground. Without wasting a second, *Troodon* swung his head down and snapped up the furry creature. It wiggled in his mouth for a moment and then went limp.

Troodon could have swallowed the animal right then, but he didn't. Instead, he trotted over to a nearby nest and dropped the

Some scientists believe that Troodon *may have been the smartest of all the dinosaurs. Combined with its sharp teeth and terrifying claws, this brain power made* Troodon *a fierce hunter.*

creature. Eight little *Troodon* gathered around and began tearing at its flesh. When they had eaten their fill, the big male swallowed up the leftovers.

CHAPTER TWO

What Is a *Troodon*?

The *Troodon* is a dinosaur that lived from about 73 million to 65 million years ago. Its name is taken from Greek words that mean "wounding tooth." Its sharp teeth had serrated (SEHR-rate-ed), or jagged, edges. They could easily rip the flesh of other animals.

From its snout to the tip of its tail, *Troodon* was 6 to 10 feet (2 to 3 meters) long. About half of that length was the dinosaur's tail. When *Troodon* stood upright, it was about 3 feet (1 m) tall. The adult **reptile** weighed between 65 and 110 pounds (30 and 50 kilograms).

Troodon*'s teeth could slice through meat as easily as a steak knife. Although not as large as meat eaters such as* Tyrannosaurus rex *(tie-RAN-uh-SAWR-uhss REX) or* Allosaurus *(AL-oh-SAWR-uhss),* Troodon *was just as deadly.*

Troodon's head was long and

While scientists believe that larger meat eaters could not move quickly due to their bulky body weight, Troodon *was smaller and was probably a fast runner.*

ended in a round snout. The dinosaur had a large mouth, and its jaws were lined with more than 100 teeth. The teeth were not long, but they were sharp, curved backwards, and zigzagged like steak knives.

Troodon had short, thin arms and long, birdlike legs. Its arms could probably rotate, or twist around. This would help it catch, tear, and hang on to smaller animals. Each hand had three long fingers ending in sharp claws.

How do scientists know that Troodon *was a good runner? Experts can estimate a dinosaur's speed by analyzing the length of its legs, its weight, and fossilized footprints.*

The dinosaur could probably run quickly with its long legs. As it ran, it pounded the ground with its long, four-toed feet. Three of these toes supported most of the *Troodon*'s weight, while the fourth was much smaller. One toe on each foot ended in a huge claw. When the animal ran, it drew these middle claws up and back so they never hit the ground.

Troodon had large eyes that were about the size of golf balls. Animals with unusually big eyes often see well in the dark. So some scientists believe *Troodon* may have hunted at night. *Troodon*'s eyes also aimed forward. Most dinosaurs had eyes that looked out to opposite sides. With forward-pointing eyes, *Troodon* could better judge distances.

The dinosaur's hearing was probably sharp, but its sense of smell may not have been as good. *Troodon*'s brain was quite large for the animal's size. For this reason, some people believe that *Troodon* was the smartest dinosaur that ever lived.

Troodon*'s large eyes probably gave it an advantage over other meat eaters that only searched for food during the day. Because* Troodon *was able to hunt when other dinosaurs were sleeping, it had less competition for its next meal.*

WHAT WAS IN THAT *TROODON* BRAIN?

Why do scientists think *Troodon* had a poor sense of smell? How can they say that a dinosaur had good eyesight? How do they know its hearing was any good? They can't test a dinosaur's senses, so where do they get such ideas?

First, scientists study the brains and skulls of living animals. Then they apply their knowledge to **extinct** animals. Scientists know that an animal's brain has different parts that do different things. For example, there's a brain part that just handles vision. In animals with very good eyesight, that brain part is large. There's also a brain part that handles odors. In animals with a sharp sense of smell, that brain part is well developed. In some cases, the large, well-developed parts appear as big bumps or bulges on the brain.

In many living animals, the skull bones form a protective cap over the brain. These bones fit snugly over the brain. Where the brain bulges out, the bony cap bulges out to make room for it.

Scientists cannot look at a dinosaur's brain. The soft brain rotted away millions of years ago. But they *can* look at the bony skull.

They can see where skull bones bulged out to leave room for large brain parts.

It seems that there are big bulges where the skull bones covered the vision part of *Troodon*'s brain. Therefore, scientists believe the dinosaur had good eyesight. The size of an animal's eye sockets also provides clues about its sense of vision.

Troodon's eye sockets are enormous compared to its skull. It might have been able to spy **prey** far away or maybe even see well at night. There are also big bony sections that protected the hearing area of *Troodon*'s brain. So scientists figure the dinosaur had good hearing. It could probably detect the slightest sounds.

CHAPTER THREE

WHO FOUND THE FIRST *TROODON*?

Ferdinand Hayden found the first *Troodon* **fossil** in 1855 in Montana. All he found at first was a single tooth. But at the time, this was a big discovery.

In the mid-1800s, dinosaurs were extremely popular, especially in Europe. Scientists in England had discovered dinosaur bones years earlier. At first, they thought the fossils were from giant elephants or rhinoceroses. Some believed they came from gigantic humans. Then scientists decided the bones were from enormous reptiles that had died out years before. One scientist came up with the word *dinosaur,* meaning "terrifying lizard." He claimed the creatures were huge, terrible lizards.

Suddenly, dinosaurs became all the rage. Newspaper headlines

In addition to being a fossil hunter, Ferdinand Hayden was also an army surgeon and a geologist (jee-OL-uh-jist). A geologist is a scientist who studies the earth's soil and rocks.

screamed out every new discovery. Museums rushed to put up dinosaur displays. People lined up by the hundreds to see the remains of those terrifying lizards.

Fossil hunting is exciting work, but it's not always easy. Searching for dinosaur bones often means detailed research and days of digging in the hot sun. The fossil dig shown here took place in Montana in the early 1900s, but scientists often must travel to faraway places such as Egypt or Mongolia.

But in America, not much was happening. Not a single dinosaur had been named. Fortunately, a scientist named Joseph Leidy became interested in fossils. He sent his friend Ferdinand Hayden out West to explore and hunt for fossils.

Hayden must have been a very energetic fossil collector. The Sioux Indians gave him the name "he who picks up rocks running," probably because he got so excited when he found fossils. Hayden came back from Montana's Judith and Missouri rivers with many fossils, including the teeth of three different dinosaurs.

Joseph Leidy knew right away that these were important finds. The next year, he wrote a paper describing one of the dinosaurs. This was a new dinosaur, never before discovered. When Leidy called it *Troodon,* it became one of the first dinosaurs named in North America.

Hayden and his team discovered quite a few amazing fossils near the Judith River in Montana. In 1992, the Judith River Dinosaur Institute was established in Malta, Montana, to help the public learn about **paleontologists** *and their work.*

JOSEPH LEIDY, A BUSY SCIENTIST

Born in Philadelphia, Pennsylvania, in 1823, Joseph Leidy (below) grew up to become a famous scientist. As a boy, he wasn't very interested in school or sports. Instead, he liked to explore the woods, fields, ponds, and rivers near his home. He also loved to draw and spent hours drawing pictures of plants and animals.

When Joseph got older, his father wanted him to be a sign painter. But his stepmother said Joseph should study medicine instead. So off he went to medical school.

In medical school, Joseph continued to study and draw animals. Soon

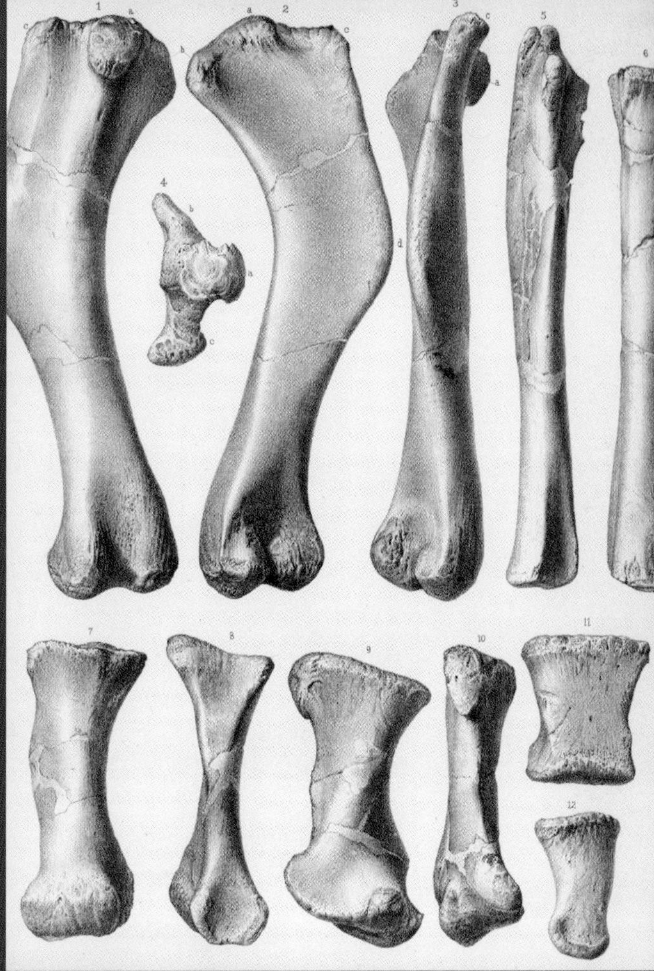

he caught the attention of some famous doctors and scientists. One scientist asked him to draw the pictures for his new book. Another one showed him how to use a rare and wonderful instrument—the microscope.

In time, Leidy became a doctor, but he remained interested in everything. He studied termites, snails, and mammals. He wrote papers about parasites—little animals that live inside the bodies of other animals. He gave speeches about **prehistoric** creatures. He wrote textbooks for college students. He collected fossils and figured out which animals they came from.

Leidy also liked to explain science to the public. He often gave talks that made everyone excited about new scientific discoveries. By the time he died at age 67, Joseph Leidy had become one of the best-known scientists in the world.

CHAPTER FOUR

What Did *Troodon* Do All the Time?

What do *most* animals do all the time? They look for food, and they eat, drink, and sleep. Adults take care of their young. Youngsters explore and play. This is probably how *Troodon* spent most of its time.

Troodon was a meat eater, or carnivore (KAR-nih-vore). The dinosaur probably spent some of its time chasing down lizards, other little reptiles, and small mammals. It may have also eaten large insects.

If it had to, *Troodon* could run quickly, using its stiff tail for balance. The dinosaur ran on its hind legs with its arms held in front or folded at its sides. Its arms could move quickly, and its hands could grasp and hold prey tightly.

This fossilized dragonfly would have seemed like a tasty treat to a Troodon. *Some prehistoric dragonflies were so large that they had a wingspan of 2 feet (70 centimeters).*

Troodon's strong jaws could clamp down on a smaller animal. Its short teeth would not pierce deeply. But they could easily shred the animal's flesh.

It is possible that Troodon *traveled in groups. Meat eaters that lived in herds usually did so to improve hunting. Plant eaters, on the other hand, traveled in herds for protection.*

Scientists have sometimes found skeletons of young and old *Troodon* all together in one place. This could mean that the dinosaurs traveled in a group. However, it might just mean that their bodies happened to wash down to the same place after they died. No one is sure. Many scientists believe that *Troodon* families stayed together at least for a while. Until the young ones could fend for themselves, they may have stayed with their parents, brothers, and sisters.

CHAPTER FIVE

Eggs by the Dozens

Not every dinosaur left eggs and nests behind, but *Troodon* did. In 1993, paleontologists found part of the skeleton of an adult *Troodon* on top of a batch of eggs. The scientists carefully

Paleontologists discovered Troodon *eggs in Montana. The eggs shown here are now housed at the National Museum of Natural History in Washington, D.C.*

Even before they were born, Troodon *babies had sharp teeth and long legs. Scientists believe young* Troodon *may have done their own hunting from the moment they hatched.*

studied the *Troodon* eggs and saw that they had babies inside them. Even before they hatched, the babies had long legs and plenty of teeth.

Paleontologists say that *Troodon* adults used dirt to build bowl-shaped nests on the ground. Once the nest was ready, the mother would lay her eggs—a process that might have taken anywhere from many hours to several weeks! A *Troodon* mother would lay two eggs at a time, until as many as 24 eggs were laid. The eggs were long and stood on end in the nest. The surrounding earth and the body of the mother or father kept the eggs warm.

Paleontologists have discovered fossilized dinosaur eggs such as the one shown here at more than 220 locations around the world.

The crocodile is a modern-day relative of Troodon. *Like their prehistoric ancestors, crocodiles also keep watch over their eggs.*

It probably took weeks for all of the eggs to hatch. Little *Troodon* babies might have been running all over the place while their younger brothers and sisters were just pecking out of their eggs. Because eggs took so long to hatch, one or both parents had to stay with the nest for at least a few weeks.

CHAPTER SIX

WHAT BECAME OF *TROODON*?

Scientists aren't exactly sure what happened to *Troodon.* They know it was among the very last dinosaurs to exist. After walking the earth for about 8 million years, the animal just disappeared.

Altogether, dinosaurs roamed the earth for about 165 million years. The first dinosaurs appeared about 230 million years ago. The last ones

Troodon *lived during the Cretaceous (kreh-TAY-shuss) period, which began 144 million years ago and lasted 79 million years.*

Scientists aren't certain what caused all the dinosaurs to die out 65 million years ago. If dinosaurs were cold blooded, their body temperatures would have been affected by the environment. A sudden change in temperature might have made it difficult for them to survive.

died out around 65 million years ago. No one knows exactly why. So far, paleontologists have found the fossils of several hundred different kinds of dinosaurs. But they've never found a clear answer as to why the dinosaurs died out.

Some of those dinosaurs probably disappeared because food became scarce. Some of them may have died because the earth became too warm or too cool. Some may have been wiped out when volcanoes spewed gases and ash, making the air difficult to breathe. Some may have disappeared after an **asteroid** hit the earth. Because everything happened so long ago, the answer might never be known.

If an asteroid hit the earth, the resulting changes in sunlight and temperature would have killed off several plants. Without anything to eat, plant-eating dinosaurs would have died out, and meat-eating dinosaurs would have soon followed.

Glossary

asteroid (ASS-tuh-roid) An asteroid is a rocky mass that is smaller than a planet and orbits the sun. Dinosaurs may have disappeared after an asteroid hit the earth.

extinct (ek-STINGKT) Something that is extinct no longer exists. The dinosaurs are now extinct.

fossil (FOSS-uhl) A fossil is the remains of an ancient plant or animal. Ferdinand Hayden found the first *Troodon* fossil in 1855.

paleontologists (PAY-lee-un-TAWL-uh-jists) Paleontologists are people who look at fossils of ancient plants and animals, and try to figure out how they lived. Paleontologists found part of the skeleton of an adult *Troodon* on top of a batch of eggs.

prehistoric (pree-hi-STOR-ik) Prehistoric refers to a time long ago, before human beings began to record history. Dinosaurs lived in prehistoric times.

prey (PRAY) Prey are animals that are hunted and eaten by other animals. *Troodon*'s good eyesight and hearing probably helped it track down prey.

reptile (REP-tile) A reptile is an animal that breathes air, has a backbone, and is usually covered with scales or plates. *Troodon* was a reptile.

Did You Know?

- Like bird eggshells, dinosaur eggshells had tiny pores, or holes, to let gases pass through them.
- Modern-day birds turn their eggs in the nest. This keeps the eggs evenly warmed and allows gases to pass through the shells. *Troodon,* however, laid its eggs upright and left them that way.
- It probably took about five years for a *Troodon* to reach adult size.
- *Troodon* had a flexible tail. It also probably had a good sense of balance. These things would have been helpful as the dinosaur ran and made quick turns.

How to Learn More

AT THE LIBRARY

Felber, Eric P., and Philip J. Currie. *A Moment in Time with Troodon.* Calgary, Alberta: Troodon Productions, Inc., 1997.

Lambert, David, Darren Naish, and Liz Wyse. *Dinosaur Encyclopedia.* New York: DK Publishing, 2001.

Lessem, Don, and Donna Braginetz (illustrator). *Troodon, the Smartest Dinosaur.* Minneapolis: Carolrhoda Books, 1995.

ON THE WEB

Visit our home page for lots of links about *Troodon*:

http://www.childsworld.com/links.html

NOTE TO PARENTS, TEACHERS, AND LIBRARIANS: We routinely verify our Web links to make sure they're safe, active sites—so encourage your readers to check them out!

PLACES TO VISIT OR CONTACT

AMERICAN MUSEUM OF NATURAL HISTORY
To view numerous dinosaur fossils, as well as the fossils of several ancient mammals
Central Park West at 79th Street
New York, NY 10024-5192
212/769-5100

CARNEGIE MUSEUM OF NATURAL HISTORY
To view a variety of dinosaur skeletons, as well as fossils related to other extinct animals
4400 Forbes Avenue
Pittsburgh, PA 15213
412/622-3131

DINOSAUR NATIONAL MONUMENT
To view a huge deposit of dinosaur bones in a natural setting
Dinosaur, CO 81610-9724
or
DINOSAUR NATIONAL MONUMENT (QUARRY)
11625 East 1500 South
Jensen, UT 84035
435/781-7700

MUSEUM OF THE ROCKIES
To see real dinosaur fossils, as well as robotic replicas
Montana State University
600 West Kagy Boulevard
Bozeman, MT 59717-2730
406/994-2251 or 406/994-DINO (3466)

NATIONAL MUSEUM OF NATURAL HISTORY (SMITHSONIAN INSTITUTION)
To see several dinosaur exhibits and special behind-the-scenes tours
10th Street and Constitution Avenue NW
Washington, DC 20560-0166
202/357-2700

The Geologic Time Scale

CAMBRIAN PERIOD

Date: 540 million to 505 million years ago
Most major animal groups appeared by the end of this period. Trilobites were common and algae became more diversified.

ORDOVICIAN PERIOD

Date: 505 million to 440 million years ago
Marine life became more diversified. Crinoids and blastoids appeared, as did corals and primitive fish. The first land plants appeared. The climate changed greatly during this period—it began as warm and moist, but temperatures ultimately dropped. Huge glaciers formed, causing sea levels to fall.

SILURIAN PERIOD

Date: 440 million to 410 million years ago
Glaciers melted, sea levels rose, and the earth's climate became more stable. Fish with jaws first appeared, as did the first freshwater fish. Plants with vascular systems developed. This means they had parts that helped them to conduct food and water.

DEVONIAN PERIOD

Date: 410 million to 360 million years ago
Fish became more diverse, as did land plants. The first trees and forests appeared at this time, and the earliest seed-bearing plants began to grow. The first land-living vertebrates and insects appeared. Fossils also reveal evidence of the first ammonites and amphibians. The climate was warm and mild.

CARBONIFEROUS PERIOD

Date: 360 million to 286 million years ago
The climate was warm and humid, but cooled toward the end of the period. Coal swamps dotted the landscape, as did a multitude of ferns. The earliest reptiles walked the earth. Pelycosaurs such as *Edaphosaurus* evolved toward the end of the Carboniferous period.

PERMIAN PERIOD

Date: 286 million to 248 million years ago
Algae, sponges and corals were common on the ocean floor. Amphibians and reptiles were also prevalent at this time, as were seed-bearing plants and conifers. However, this period ended with the largest mass extinction on earth. This may have been caused by volcanic activity or the formation of glaciers and the lowering of sea levels.

TRIASSIC PERIOD

Date: 248 million to 208 million years ago
The climate during this period was warm and dry. The first true mammals appeared, as did frogs, salamanders, and lizards. Evergreen trees made up much of the plant life. The first dinosaurs, including *Coelophysis*, walked the earth. In the skies, pterosaurs became the earliest winged reptiles to take flight. In the seas, ichthyosaurs and plesiosaurs made their appearance.

JURASSIC PERIOD

Date: 208 million to 144 million years ago
The climate of the Jurassic period was warm and moist. The first birds appeared at this time, and plant life was more diverse and widespread. Although dinosaurs didn't even exist in the beginning of the Triassic period, they ruled the earth by Jurassic times. *Allosaurus, Apatosaurus, Archaeopteryx, Brachiosaurus, Compsognathus, Diplodocus, Ichthyosaurus, Plesiosaurus,* and *Stegosaurus* were just a few of the prehistoric creatures that lived during this period.

CRETACEOUS PERIOD

Date: 144 million to 65 million years ago
The climate of the Cretaceous period was fairly mild. Many modern plants developed, including those with flowers. With flowering plants came a greater diversity of insect life. Birds further developed into two types: flying and flightless. Prehistoric creatures such as *Ankylosaurus, Edmontosaurus, Iguanodon, Maiasaura, Oviraptor, Psittacosaurus, Spinosaurus, Triceratops, Troodon, Tyrannosaurus rex,* and *Velociraptor* all existed during this period. At the end of the Cretaceous period came a great mass extinction that wiped out the dinosaurs, along with many other groups of animals.

TERTIARY PERIOD

Date: 65 million to 1.8 million years ago
Mammals were extremely diversified at this time, and modern-day creatures such as horses, dogs, cats, bears, and whales developed.

QUATERNARY PERIOD

Date: 1.8 million years ago to today
Temperatures continued to drop during this period. Several periods of glacial development led to what is known today as the Ice Age. Prehistoric creatures such as glyptodonts, mammoths, mastodons, *Megatherium*, and sabre-toothed cats roamed the earth. A mass extinction of these animals occurred approximately 10,000 years ago. The first human beings evolved during the Quaternary period.

Index

About the Author

Susan H. Gray has bachelor's and master's degrees in zoology and has taught college-level courses in biology. She first fell in love with fossil hunting while studying paleontology in college. In her 25 years as an author, she has written many articles for scientists and researchers, and many science books for children. Susan enjoys gardening, traveling, and playing the piano. She and her husband, Michael, live in Cabot, Arkansas.